Introduction

There is an unfortunate need for a book on a diet for those who are lacking iron. Anemia is a common problem and can plague many types of people. When we are lacking in iron, it can sometimes seem like life is simply excessively hard. We are drained and injury and hurt without any problem. That, yet it very well may be challenging to focus and recall the things that we are told and undertakings that should be accomplished.

All of these outcomes of living without sufficient iron in the circulation system can prompt genuine medical problems, so it is a higher priority than at any other time to start to take action.

If you have as of now been determined to have sickliness, you have been living with low iron for a really long time. Assuming you are leaving on a way of life change like veganism or vegetarianism, or you basically have removed wellsprings of iron from your eating routine for individual reasons, enhancing iron is a major advance to remain healthy.

But for what reason would we be able to simply pop an iron pill and move on?

Unfortunately, studies have shown that enhancements are not generally sufficient ways for our bodies to get supplements. That, yet taking iron enhancements won't ensure that our bodies even assimilate the iron that we take.

With that as a top priority, we will set out upon an excursion to find precisely how it affects our bodies to live without iron in our eating regimens and how we might guarantee that we are getting satisfactory nutrition.

At the finish of the book, a couple of plans will be presented for the individuals who are new to an existence with low iron in their weight control plans, alongside ideas for individuals who have been living with sickliness for quite a while. It's opportunity to start to take care of all of this and this book will show you how.

WHAT IS IRON AND WHY DO I NEED IT?

Most of us understand that having heavy metals in the body can be a very bad thing. For example, studies have proven that an accumulation of heavy metals in the bloodstream, such as aluminum, are connected with neurological issues, including, yet not restricted to, Alzheimer's illness and dementia. So for what reason is it so vital to ensure that we are getting enough of the weighty metal iron in our bodies?

Actually iron is vital for practically all living things to work. Everyone, from people to elephants to microscopic organisms, has some dependence on iron. Iron is a bio-component that assists electrons with moving all through the body, and that's only the tip of the iceberg or less assumes a part in where electrons go and what they do.

Iron: Ferrous State and Ferric State

There are two unique conditions of iron. The first is the ferrous state. In a ferrous state, iron gives electrons and offers them up to where they should be. In the other, the ferric state, iron acknowledges electrons from different spots. Regardless of whether iron is going about as an electron contributor or an acceptor, it assumes a pivotal part in intervening the responses of compounds by either oxidizing them, transforming them into rust, or diminishing the enzymes.

Our bodies don't really rust, yet they truly do have a dependence on this bio-component. The body needs iron to assist with moving oxygen all through the body and to invigorate cells with energy. This interaction is known as cell respiration.

Recommended Daily Iron Intake

Wow, you might think, perhaps I ought to go out and eat only iron!

That would be a mix-up. Iron is however valuable as it could be hazardous.

To keep away from harmfulness, it is prescribed to get just the day by day measure of iron suggested by nutritionists. Iron admission is variable relying upon your age and sex.

Currently, the suggested worth of iron admission is as follows:

- Females seven to a year old - 11mg
- Males seven to a year old - 11mg
- Females one to three years of age - 7mg
- Males one to three years of age - 7 mg
- Females four to eight years of age - 10mg
- Males four to eight years of age - 10 mg
- Females nine to 13 years of age - 8 mg
- Males nine to 13 years of age - 8 mg
- Females 14-18 years of age - 15mg
- Males 14-18 years of age - 11mg
- Females 19-50 years of age - 18mg
- Males 19-50 years of age - 8mg
- Females 51 years and more established - 8mg
- Males 51 years and more seasoned - 8mg

Women who are pregnant require 27mg of iron admission and if lactating, ought to have 10 mg assuming that they are between 14-18 years of age, or 9mg in the event that they are 19-50 years old.

Iron and Hemoglobin

The main capacity of iron in a human body is to carry oxygen into the body's tissues. It attempts to convey air from the lungs to the muscles and ligaments utilizing the ferrous and ferric states momentarily talked about in the previous section. Without iron in the hemoglobin, the component that makes this transfer possible in the body, then we start to see some problems.

Hemoglobin is a component related with the blood since it is found in red platelets. Oxygen is brought through the body in these platelets through the hemoglobin from the lungs. As it gives oxygen to the body's muscles and tissues, it trades the oxygen for carbon dioxide. Whenever it gets once again to the lungs, it carries that carbon dioxide back with it and stores it in the lungs as well.

Most of us are likely acquainted with the way that we take in oxygen and bring out carbon dioxide. That interaction is a fundamental cycle for the body and it occurs on a tiny as well as naturally visible scale for this situation. The oxygen we take in is moved from the lungs on the hemoglobin. The hemoglobin brings it through the body's circulation system and stores it where it should be to work the best. At the point when it stores the oxygen in the tissues, it is traded with carbon dioxide. The carbon dioxide is then removed out of the body from the lungs.

It is a consistent cycle that permits our bodies to be really sound. Without it, we go into risky territory.

What Is Hemoglobin?

Hemoglobin is framed from four protein atoms that make up a chain. In the chain are alpha-globulin and beta-globulin. For the most part, beta-globulin chains are just shaped as we develop and are seldom found in infants and youthful children.

Hemoglobin is so named in light of the compound heme. This is the place where the iron iota is situated inside the chain so we can move oxygen all through our body. Without hemoglobin, our platelets wouldn't have the uniform state of a sound platelet, so it is feasible for platelets to become deformed and run into versatility issues.

By and large, we need to see a particular scope of hemoglobin in the platelets and on the off chance that that reach goes excessively high or excessively low, there are issues. Generally, the issue is too minimal iron being consumed by the body and blocking the improvement of hemoglobin. Similarly as with most estimations, age and sex assume a part in deciding the favored measure of hemoglobin that ought to be found in the body.

It is definitely not a careful number since all research centers might have various principles of estimation, so results might fluctuate. But these are the most approximate amounts of hemoglobin that should be present in the body at any given time. Assuming these numbers are excessively low or excessively high, issues can arise.

Pregnant ladies ought to be particularly cautious for this situation on the grounds that a lot of hemoglobin could bring about stillbirths, while insufficient hemoglobin could make children be conceived rashly or underweight. Along these lines, pregnant ladies should ensure that they are keeping hemoglobin levels even: not excessively high, nor too low.

The scope of hemoglobin favored is as follows:

•Infants (male and female) under seven days old enough: 17-22gm per hundred milliliters

•Infants (male and female) multi week old: 15-20gm per hundred milliliters

•Infants (male and female) one month old: 11-15gm per hundred milliliters

•Children (male and female) one month old through 18 years of age: 11-13gm per hundred milliliters

•Adult guys 18-40 years old: 14-18gm per hundred milliliters

•Adult females 18-40 years old: 12-15gm per hundred milliliters

•Males past middle age: 12.4-14.9gm per hundred milliliters

•Females past middle age: 11.7gm-13.8gm per hundred milliliters

Overall, it very well may be essential to have the legitimate degrees of hemoglobin. Assuming you fall above or underneath the standard degrees of hemoglobin in the body, that implies that you are inadequate in iron or getting an excessive amount of iron, and may wind up having
medical issues as a result.

What Happens When Red Blood Cells Lack Hemoglobin?

Our bodies will by and large create red platelets, yet whether or not these platelets contain hemoglobin is actually an issue of how much iron we are getting in the body. Whenever we aren't getting the perfect proportion of iron, the protein compound known as hemoglobin will turn into significantly more difficult to find. This implies that our bodies will have some issues.

As referenced already, without hemoglobin, our tissues and muscles wouldn't get the oxygen fundamental in guaranteeing our great wellbeing. When our stores of iron have been adequately drained, our bodies will likewise start to deliver less red platelets. This can be an issue. That, yet when the body can deliver red platelets, these cells will be deficient in the vital compound hemoglobin.

To sum up, when our body has been exhausted of our iron stores and starts to create less platelets, and those platelets are inadequate in the hemoglobin vital in keeping our bodies sound and working, a particular issue can emerge known as pallor. Weakness can have a wide range of causes, iron lack being one of the most well-known. This torment will be talked about in a later chapter.

Iron Deficiency and Excess Iron In the Body

Lack of iron can be an extremely perilous difficulty. Yet, what a great many people don't understand is that low iron in the body isn't simply an issue actually. It tends to be an issue mentally as well.

Unfortunately, experiencing low iron is related with intricacies that range anyplace from suspicion to pallor. Since iron is so critical to our physical and psychological wellness, it is vital to ensure that we are getting sufficient iron in our diet.

However, there is likewise such an incredible concept as getting a lot of iron in the body. An overdose of something that is otherwise good isn't in every case essentially the response. Indeed, overabundance iron in the body can likewise cause issues. Since it is a weighty metal, we must be mindful so as to ensure we keep up with legitimate iron levels or face genuine consequences.

Heme and Non- Heme Iron

The iron we get from our eating routine comes in two structures. These incorporate heme iron and non-heme iron. The distinctions in these two sorts of iron are the sources from which they are inferred. Heme iron is gotten from creature sources, like fish, red meat, and poultry. Non-heme iron comes from plants and food sources that are invigorated with iron.

While heme iron is for the most part accepted to be simpler for the body to assimilate and use, it is additionally viewed as somewhat more hazardous. Wellbeing impacts of heme iron incorporate expanded hazard of issues like coronary illness, stroke, and malignant growth. It might likewise contrarily affect the metabolic system.

Sometimes, an excess of meat utilization can adversely affect the body, and even lead to difficulties further down the road related with an over-burden of iron in the body. It is critical to eat a supplement rich and various eating regimen to stay away from entanglements with heme and non-heme iron in the body.

How Does Iron Deficiency Happen?

Unfortunately, iron inadequacy is perhaps the most widely recognized nutrient and mineral insufficiency known to North America. It is extremely simple, and its significance is seldom anxious when sustenance is talked about. In any case, having an absence of hemoglobin in the body can be extremely risky to our psychological and physical functioning.

Sometimes, we could foster a lack of iron since we have a remarkable hemoglobin structure. Whenever our hemoglobin structures are strange, this can prompt a lack of iron in our blood. For instance, individuals with thalassemia and sickle cell sickliness may see that they are inclined to iron deficiencies.

Another way lacks of iron could create is assuming we are in appalling mishaps or have medical problems that lead to an enormous amount of blood lost. We might lose blood from an auto collision, kidney disappointment, or some other sort of horrible injury. Now and then, it's anything but a mishap by any stretch of the imagination, and the explanation we have lost a ton of blood is on the grounds that we have decided to give blood consistently. Anything that the explanation, huge amounts of blood misfortune can be a huge reason for lack of iron anemia.

Women who are pregnant and young ladies with weighty periods are likewise at high gamble. Pregnant ladies, specifically, are powerless as their bodies go through a progression of actual changes, including doling out blood to the uterus, where they use it to help the development of the infants within them. But as mentioned previously, that makes it all the more important to have hemoglobin levels as close to normal as possible.

Sometimes, we essentially struggle retaining iron, regardless of the amount we eat. At the point when this is the situation, it is frequently because of medical conditions or gastrointestinal medical procedures. For instance, individuals with celiac illness regularly have just a confined measure of iron that the body can ingest at one time.

Cancer can likewise be a reason for lack of iron. Whenever red platelet amalgamation is stifled by drugs that are a piece of chemotherapy therapies or bone marrow is supplanted by dangerous cells, these can both drain iron in the framework. It's an appalling aftereffect of an as of now tragic disease.

Another issue that can prompt lack of iron weakness is inside dying. It sounds exceptionally terrifying, and without a doubt can be. Things like ulcers and polyps are normal reasons for inner dying. Iron deficiency can likewise happen if over-the-counter torment meds like ibuprofen are much of the time utilized. Sadly, while they guarantee to assist us with feeling good, a typical symptom of utilizing these "meds" is draining in the stomach. Uterine fibroids have likewise been analyzed as a reason for lack of iron paleness. Whenever these fibroids create, they can cause serious agony in the midsection and a weighty feminine stream, which has likewise been connected to anemia.

Finally, and perhaps most regularly, a deficient eating regimen can be the consequence of lack of iron. In the event that the body doesn't get sufficient vitamin B12, folate, or iron, it can make it truly challenging for iron to stay in the body or be

consumed and used for its legitimate function.

Symptoms of Iron Deficiency

Sometimes we don't understand there is an issue until it is past the point of no return. Notwithstanding, on the off chance that we are tenacious, it is feasible to discover advance notice indications of lack of iron before they turn excessively intense. In any case, iron lack is a difficulty that can be treated effortlessly by fusing way of life changes that make it more straightforward for our bodies to get and assimilate iron. Here are an indications of lack of iron to watch out for.

•Lethargy

•Fatigue

•Less viable invulnerable framework functioning

- Inflammation of the tongue
- Fluctuations in body temperature
- Fragile finger and toe nails
- Decreased execution, regardless of whether at school or work
- Slow cerebrum development
- Pale skin
- Strange desires, for example, the longing to eat dirt
- Irregular heartbeat
- Shortness of breath
- Strange disturbing sensations in the legs
- Swelling of the tongue
- Sore tongue
- Difficulty in warming furthest points, like hands and feet
- Decreased mental functioning
- Difficulties in doing physical work
- Memory misfortune and diminished capacity of the memory
- Decreased mental functions

As you can tell, these can be not kidding issues that ought to be tended to immediately. This is particularly obvious if pregnant. Moms with lacks of iron have a more prominent possibility bringing forth little children with lower life expectancies.

Symptoms of Excess Iron

Getting an excessive amount of iron is generally not an issue that the vast majority talk frequently about. For the most part, paleness is the superstar with regards to discussions regarding iron. In any case, it is feasible for abundance iron to develop in the framework, and when an individual arrives at the age of 40 or more, complexities from developed iron in the framework may surface.

Symptoms of overabundance iron, albeit inconspicuous, might be noted early. These side effects include:

•Incontinence or successive urination

•Joint pain

•Fatigue

•Lethargy

•Tiredness

•Weight loss

•Difficulty performing physical work

If indications of abundance iron are gotten early, you might be determined to have overabundance iron in the blood, a condition known as hemochromatosis. Hemochromatosis will be examined further in a later section.

Iron Deficiency and Mental Health

Sometimes we might have a lack of iron and don't have any acquaintance with it. This can make mental reactions our inadequacy that may somehow be ascribed to outer variables and aggravations when as a general rule, it is an absence of iron that is adding to these wellbeing problems.

Mental and enthusiastic inconveniences of low iron in the body are frequently disregarded. Nonetheless, iron inadequacy can frequently add to discouragement, nervousness, and different troubles in mental working. On the off chance that you are not getting sufficient iron, or your body isn't engrossing iron as expected, you might be at risk.

Coming up next are a portion of the psychological and enthusiastic inconveniences that can be related with an iron deficiency:

•Depression

•Anxiety

•Irritability

•Extreme fatigue

•Appetite loss

- Panic attacks
- Insomnia
- Chest tightness
- Irregular heartbeat
- Mood swings
- Helplessness
- Sadness
- Irregular heart rhythms
- Visual disturbances
- Headaches
- Feelings of dread
- Preoccupation with death or dying
- Muscle weakness
- Issues gulping/choking
- Restless leg syndrome
- Feelings of flimsiness/vertigo
- Dizziness
- Motion sickness
- Inability to focus
- Difficulty perusing and concentrating
- Difficulty finishing basic tasks
- Stress

Overall, the psychological cost that a lack of iron can have on the body is outrageous. It tends to very disappoint to live with the physical and mental side effects of a lack of iron. On the off chance that you speculate you have low iron, visit a specialist at the earliest opportunity, or keep perusing on to track down ways of curing this burden and start to turn your life around to refocus when possible.

IRON DEFICIENCY ANEMIA: WHAT IT IS AND HOW TO COPE WITH AND PREVENT IT

Iron deficiency anemia is the specific title for people whose bodies are lacking in red blood cells and hemoglobin because of an iron deficiency. This particular ailment is the most common anemia issue and can sometimes be brought on by decisions that we make on a daily basis. Little things, like the choices we make in our diet, can play a big role when it comes to our health, and we often don't realize just how much power we have over how we feel.

Sometimes the reason for lack of iron sickliness can be straightforward, like weighty blood misfortune during a lady's monthly cycle. Ladies who experience blood misfortune during pregnancy may likewise foster this particular sort of anemia.

For the most part, iron inadequacy paleness is certifiably not a perilous condition. Notwithstanding that, there are many types of weakness that require exceptional consideration. No matter what the way that a slight lack of iron isn't viewed as unsafe, many individuals don't understand that they are experiencing this condition and when left untreated it can become risky. Due to the significant capacity of iron, assuming hemoglobin is diminished in the red platelets, it implies that the heart needs to work harder to disperse oxygen all through the body.

Unfortunately, this can prompt a sporadic heartbeat now and again or an developed heart in others. Both of these represent a genuine wellbeing hazard and whenever left untreated, they could make cardiovascular breakdown happen. This is the point at which a lack of iron goes from being badly arranged to being lethal.

How to Prevent Iron Deficiency Anemia

It is conceivable that assuming you are perusing this book, you are now experiencing lack of iron weakness. Whether or not you have effectively been determined to have frailty or you are essentially stressed over carrying on with a way of life that is low in iron, there are ways that you can try to keep lack of iron sickliness from happening to you, or deteriorating assuming it as of now has happened.

The principal method for forestalling lack of iron paleness appears to be genuinely natural. Just eat more iron. There is a section in this book altogether devoted to press rich food sources. Have a go at fusing these food sources into your eating regimen consistently and you will be nearer to keeping sickliness from happening to you or deteriorating.

The second method for forestalling lack of iron weakness is to eat food varieties that help the assimilation of iron. Whether or not we are eating sufficient iron, there are different variables at play with regards to the retention of iron in our bodies. On the off chance that our bodies aren't equipped for engrossing an adequate number of iron, that boils down to the food sources that we are eating and different supplements we might be lacking in, like B12 and folates. This is particularly normal in veggie lover and vegan eats less. Diving deeper into food sources that help iron assimilation in the body is critical, and an entire section will be committed to these food varieties as well.

The third method for guaranteeing that lack of iron frailty passes you by is to consolidate devouring iron with eating L-ascorbic acid. L-ascorbic acid is one of the numerous supplements that our bodies need a solid stock of, and this is exceptionally obvious with regards to the assimilation of iron. Eating iron-rich food sources, like spinach, with L-ascorbic acid rich food sources, like oranges, is an extraordinary method for preparing sure that our bodies are to retain the iron that we give it.

What to Do When Diagnosed With Iron Deficiency Anemia

Living with any sort of clinical issue can be truly challenging, particularly when these issues expect changes to be made to our day by day schedules and diets. Sadly, that is continuously going to be the situation when our bodies are inadequate in nutrients and supplements. Without these supplements, our bodies will progressively become more vulnerable and confusions may arise.

When you are authoritatively determined to have lack of iron sickliness, it is essential to find out about the extent of the issue. Assuming you have been living on a tight eating routine that is seriously ailing in iron for a long time, entanglements might emerge from that, and these complexities ought to be managed through clinical consideration. Try not to endeavor to self-treat lack of iron pallor, as we are for the most part unique and our bodies require explicit nutrients and minerals to work properly.

If you are determined to have lack of iron frailty, there are a couple of steps that you should take right away. The first is to talk with your PCP about fitting enhancements, for iron as well as for vitamin B12 and folates also, as these inadequacies are regularly found close by the lack of iron and come inseparably. Once you have discussed the proper supplementation that is right for you, then you are going to be responsible for improving your diet and making sure that you are getting enough vitamins and minerals to maintain a healthy lifestyle.

It is vital that you find out as much regarding the particular sort of sickliness that you have. Be transparent with your PCPs, as they will regularly keep treatment until they have pinpointed the hidden reason for your illness. At the point when they have a smart thought of what is causing your issues, really at that time will they feel happy with settling on a line of activity to assist you with treating your iron deficiency.

When to Consult a Doctor

Unfortunately, frailty that can be fixed and forestalled simply through the eating regimen isn't the main kind of sickliness that can create. While the ideas referenced above are extraordinary ways of assisting iron with entering the body, there are a few times when clinical mediation is expected to treat your particular kind of anemia.

While diet is a critical element in living with pallor, there are times when your particular clinical necessities won't be fixed by diet alone. For instance, those with celiac infection or other gastrointestinal sicknesses will require the assistance of a specialist to get legitimate nutrition.

Other sorts of pallor that ought to be managed by an accomplished clinical consideration professional who is knowledgeable on your particular case incorporate Crohn's illness, aplastic frailty, disease initiated iron deficiency, and hemolytic paleness. These types of paleness require clinical consideration and the data in this book ought not be utilized as a substitute for mindful clinical advice.

Coping With Iron Deficiency Anemia

Depending on how far along it is, the ordinary agreement is that sickliness is something that can be handily treated. However, complications from long-term anemia can be a little bit more dangerous, such as heart growth or irregular heartbeats.

Fortunately, the vast majority get frailty almost immediately, and adapting to it very well may be simple. More often than not, enhancements will be involved, and their need might endure anyplace from a couple of months to a year or more, contingent upon what your PCP suggests. It is essential to adhere to guidelines and give close consideration to any manifestations that the iron enhancements you are taking reason you to have, as it can become hazardous to put an excessive amount of iron in the body.

When you are taking enhancements, try to routinely talk with your primary care physician and inquire as to whether you wind up experiencing gastrointestinal misery or opposite secondary effects from the enhancements. While you are taking the enhancements, attempt to start eating iron-rich food varieties and food varieties that will uphold the retention of iron in your system.

Listen cautiously to any orders and proposals given to you by your primary care physician and follow them until you are free. Now and again, you might wind up expecting to get blood or an IV to assist manage extreme lack of iron. Lack of iron weakness isn't dependably a difficult issue, yet when it perseveres for a really long time, inconveniences might become serious. Do whatever is important to conquer these hindrances and equilibrium out your lack once and for all.

ALL YOU NEED TO KNOW ABOUT IRON SUPPLEMENTS

The unfortunate fact of the matter is that with any diet that is low in anything, supplements are going to be the best way to receive more nutrition. It is almost guaranteed that if you are struggling with iron deficiency anemia, you will be prescribed an iron supplement to help you to cope with this inadequacy in your diet. However, there are many questions and concerns that you might have when it comes to taking a supplement to improve your health. This chapter will go through the most common questions related with iron supplements.

Ferrous Versus Ferric Iron

It is difficult to tell which kind of iron enhancement you should be taking without clinical mediation. There are two fundamental kinds of iron enhancements accessible and keeping in mind that each have their own advantages, it is vital to counsel a specialist prior to endeavoring to treat lack of iron paleness with supplements.

Most of iron enhancements are made of ferrous iron, just on the grounds that it is somewhat more straightforward on the body and can be ingested better. There are three subcategories of ferrous iron. Ferrous fumarate, ferrous sulfate, and ferrous gluconate are most frequently endorsed to the individuals who are experiencing a lack of iron. This is on the grounds that they are by and large the quickest method for bringing iron into a body that is experiencing iron deficiency.

Unfortunately for our bodies, ferric iron is on rare occasions endorsed in light of the fact that it doesn't get assimilated as without any problem. Our bodies struggle separating ferric iron into the structure that is simplest for us to retain - ferrous iron. This might be hazardous in light of the fact that a failure to separate iron can prompt iron harming. On the off chance that you are endorsed ferric iron, supplements made with iron citrate are suggested, as this is the least demanding type of ferric iron for our bodies to utilize.

What to Look for in Ferrous Iron Supplements

Ferrous iron enhancements come in fluid structure, containers, tablets, drops, and broadened discharge recipes. It is essential to take a gander at the "Basic Iron" sum in an iron enhancement prior to settling on which is ideal for you. It is for the most part concurred that grown-ups with lack of iron pallor need to get somewhere close to 60 and 200 milligrams of natural iron.

How to Take Iron Supplements

Whenever leaving upon another kind of medicine, there are a few rules and decides that will apply. Iron enhancements are no special case. To get the full advantage of your iron enhancement, there are a couple of rules to follow.

First of all, never take iron enhancements with tea, milk, or other dairy items. Tragically, calcium adversely affects iron ingestion and can forestall the ideal impacts of iron supplementation. It is additionally significant not to join iron with acid neutralizers for comparable reasons. You should make a point to time the admission of calcium and acid neutralizers so you don't take them inside two hours of taking your iron supplements.

Instead of taking your iron with a glass of milk, it is suggested that you take your iron enhancement with squeezed orange. Squeezed orange is loaded with L-ascorbic acid, which supports the retention of iron in the body. This blend will guarantee that as a significant part of the iron enhancement makes it into your body as possible.

It is likewise suggested that iron enhancements be taken on a vacant stomach. Iron enhancements might cause a tad of stomach upset, so assuming you truly need to, you could take iron enhancements with a slice of bread. Nonetheless, the guideline is to ensure you haven't eaten somewhere around two hours prior to taking your iron enhancement. This guarantee that your body is getting however much iron from the enhancement as could reasonably be expected. Taking enhancements with food can diminish how much iron consumed by up to 60%. This will definitely bring about a more extended term of expecting to take iron supplements.

If you are taking your iron enhancement in fluid structure, ensure that you are blending it completely in your beverage and drinking it with a straw. Unfortunately, iron supplements tend to stain the teeth, even darkening the stool, so it is recommended that a straw is used when taking the supplement. Make certain to clean your teeth completely subsequent to drinking a fluid enhancement to forestall staining the teeth.

Make sure that you are polishing off a ton of fluids when you take your iron enhancements. The fluids will assist with offing set the normal issue of stoppage that happens with iron enhancements. Over-the-counter stool conditioners are protected to combine with iron enhancements assuming this is an issue for you.

Side Effects of Iron Supplements

As with anything, iron enhancements can some of the time be hazardous, especially assuming that they are taken in dosages that are excessively huge for your body to assimilate appropriately. For this reason it is so vital to have a relationship with a mindful and capable clinical specialist during the span of treatment for an iron deficiency.

Side impacts of iron enhancements fluctuate on the awkward to the limit. It is normal for stool to look dim, even dark, while taking these enhancements, yet it is perilous assuming you notice that stool has blood in it or is tar-like for all intents and purposes. Counsel your primary care physician regarding this right away and inquire as to whether these side effects happen. You should also mention if you have experienced symptoms such as nausea or stomach upset upon the consumption of iron supplements.

More risky issues might happen on the off chance that you are taking an excessive amount of iron for your
body to deal with. For instance, you can start to feel hot or experience the ill effects of cerebral pains, debilitated beat, low circulatory strain, chills, and unsteadiness. Liquid might start to develop in your lungs and it is even conceivable to go into a state of extreme lethargy assuming you glut on iron enhancements. This hazard is increased for the individuals who experience the ill effects of hemochromatosis, an innate condition that makes the body take in definitely more iron than it needs. Be cautious and consistently keep your PCP on top of it prior to settling on choices about utilization of iron supplements.

How Long Will It Take for Supplements to Make a Difference?

When we understand that we have an inadequacy, it is generally disturbing an adequate number of that we desire to track down a prompt fix. We might even feel eager to fix the issue immediately and feel like the time it takes to recuperate isn't quick enough.

However, it can invest in some opportunity for the body to start creating the legitimate measure of hemoglobin that it needs to deliver enormous, sound red platelets that can convey sufficient oxygen to the body. This is particularly obvious in the event that you have been frail for quite a while without determination or treatment. Persistence is the situation with regards to treating anemia.

If the weakness isn't excessively outrageous, iron enhancements might have the option to start to execute new red cell development and flow soon. When that starts to occur, upon the underlying gathering of the iron enhancements, hemoglobin should begin to ascend in merely a few weeks.

Depending on the seriousness of your sickliness, therapy might take just two months before the body's red platelet count and the nature of the hemoglobin are back to ordinary. Nonetheless, supplements stay a urgent piece of the treatment interaction for as long as two months afterward, just to ensure the body has sufficient iron put away for sometime later. It is essential to ensure that the body will not turn out to be effortlessly exhausted again.

FOODS THAT SUPPORT THE ABSORPTION OF IRON

Oftentimes, an iron deficiency doesn't happen alone. There are many reasons the body might not be receiving enough iron, but if the cause of this complication is dietary, there are other things that need to be taken into thought before the issue can be completely managed with.

In request for the body to assimilate the legitimate measure of iron, different supplements should be in full stock in the body and capable and able to take care of their responsibilities in helping iron ingestion. Without these nutrients and minerals present in the body, there can be complexities that might delay lack of iron sickliness and make it harder for the body to recover.

All of the accompanying supplements ought to be thought about while endeavoring to treat lack of iron anemia:

•Vitamin C

•Folates

•Vitamin B12

Without the presence of these nutrients and minerals in the body, iron ingestion will be troublesome, if not impossible.

Vitamin B 12 and Iron Absorption

Vitamin B12 and iron share a great deal practically speaking. They are both critical components with regards to the creation of sound red platelets and mind work. Without vitamin B12, the body can experience both actually and intellectually. If long haul exhaustion of vitamin B12 turns into an issue, it can cause serious sickliness and neurological problems.

Lack of vitamin B12 and iron insufficiency are regularly connected, and side effects of a lack of vitamin B12 will be examined in later parts including veggie lover and vegan slims down, as this particular issue is generally normal for individuals who cut meat out of their eating regimens. Regularly, vitamin B12 and iron are matched together in creature based food sources, so it is phenomenal for individuals who eat sufficient meat to generally disapprove of getting sufficient nutrient B12.

However, inadequacies might happen in the event that somebody experiences hardships in their stomach related frameworks. Once in a while it is additionally difficult for the body to assimilate fluid types of vitamin B12. Individuals taking a few meds or living with celiac sickness, incendiary inside infection, malicious frailty, pancreas illness, or other immune system problems are more inclined to experiencing perilous vitamin B12 deficiencies.

Folates and Iron Absorption

Folates are associated with vitamin B12. They are off-shoots of the B-complex nutrients that are fundamental in helping metabolic capacities in the body. Without enough folates in the body, iron assimilation is restricted and, if untreated, can be deadly. Without enough B12 and folates in the body, malicious frailty might create. This is significantly more risky than the development of iron-lacking pallor and includes bigger than-normal red platelets. Lacks can generally be effortlessly treated with supplements.

Vitamin C and Iron Absorption

As referenced already, L-ascorbic acid is normally exceptionally accommodating in helping with the treatment of iron-inadequate sickliness. The vast majority of us don't have a need of

L-ascorbic acid, for all intents and purposes in numerous normal food staples in North America. It is not difficult to track down L-ascorbic acid, regardless of whether one follows a plant-based diet or an eating routine established in the utilization of animals.

Every so often, a L-ascorbic acid insufficiency might happen, in light of the fact that our bodies don't normally create this fundamental nutrient. Without L-ascorbic acid, it is hard for our bodies to fix themselves, and may prompt unfortunate bones, including teeth and ligament. The skin is likewise impacted by L-ascorbic acid and may become undesirable without legitimate measures of this nutrient in the diet.

The ascorbic corrosive that is available in L-ascorbic acid is fundamental in upgrading iron assimilation. This is particularly evident in instances of ferrous iron while being less viable in the ingestion of ferric corrosive in the body. It is accepted that ill-advised capacity and treatment of L-ascorbic acid items might diminish the proficiency in utilizing ascorbic corrosive to treat lack of iron sickliness. Notwithstanding, L-ascorbic acid remaining parts a basic part in the retention of iron in the body.

Foods That Assist in the Absorption of Iron

It is obviously vital to keep a shifted diet that is plentiful in L-ascorbic acid, folates, vitamin B12, and iron for the solid working of the body and psyche. Along these lines, ensure that your body is never ailing in food varieties rich in these nutrients.

Foods that guide in the retention of iron in the body incorporate the following:

•Strawberries

•Cherries

•Citrus natural products (oranges, grapefruit, lemons, limes, etc.)

•Papaya

•Kiwi

•Blackcurrant

•Bell peppers

•Guava

•Brussels sprouts

•Melons

•Dark verdant greens

•Broccoli

•Amalaki fruit

•Cauliflower

•Tomatoes

•Cilantro

•Chives

•Thyme

•Basil

•Parsley

- Eggs
- Red meat
- Shellfish
- Fish
- Poultry
- Vitamin B12 sustained foods
- Crab
- Edamame
- Black looked at peas
- Lentils
- Spinach
- Asparagus
- Romaine lettuce
- Avocado
- Mango
- Broccoli
- Wheat bread

All of these food sources have levels of either L-ascorbic acid, vitamin B12, folates, or mixes of these nutrients that help the body in engrossing iron. Lacks of any of these nutrients can be exceptionally perilous to the framework. Assuming you presume you might have an inadequacy, read on through the part committed to veggie lovers and vegans to find out more and counsel your doctor.

IRON-RICH FOODS

It may seem obvious by now that eating foods that are rich in iron is a great way to improve the amount of iron consumed in an otherwise low-iron diet. However, this seemingly intuitive knowledge may be difficult for many, particularly those who follow a plant-based diet or lifestyle. While it can be dangerous to lack iron because of dietary preferences, it is still possible to receive adequate amounts of iron if you are persistent and devoted to meeting your wellbeing

needs. Food varieties that are wealthy

in iron include:

- Organ meats
- Lamb
- Dark meat chicken
- Pork
- Tofu
- Apricots
- Egg yolks
- Legumes
- Beans
- Pumpkin seeds
- Tuna
- Sardines
- Leafy greens
- Spinach
- Collard greens
- Kale
- Oysters
- Shellfish

- Halibut
- Salmon
- Fish
- Red meat
- Raisins
- Poultry
- Chicken
- Turkey
- Whole grains
- Amaranth
- Quinoa
- Iron-invigorated breads and cereals
- Prunes
- Dark chocolate
- Potatoes

Without ordinary utilization of iron-rich food sources and the food varieties that make it workable for our bodies to ingest iron, it tends to be extremely challenging for us to live a

even way of life. Many issues might emerge because of lacks, and of any of the things that might convolute iron admission in the body can be perilous. Along these lines, you ought to be certain all of the time to counsel your PCP or nutritionist prior to taking on another eating regimen or then again assuming you feel that you are in danger of dietary lacks. Long haul lacks in any of the nutrients or minerals referenced in this book can prompt genuine and in some cases deep rooted wellbeing results. It is better 100% of the time to be exhaustive and very much informed prior to taking on a tight eating routine that could be possibly risky to your health.

LIFESTYLE CHANGES THAT CAN IMPROVE IRON INTAKE

While it can seem daunting to get enough iron in the diet, particularly if you have chosen a diet that is low in iron or you have a difficult time absorbing iron due to other health issues, there are ways that you can start to enhance iron in your day to day existence by simplifying a couple changes.

First, attempt to consume less espresso, tea, and other stimulated items. Sadly, these items can make it considerably more hard for our bodies to assimilate iron. While it might appear to be troublesome, particularly assuming you have fostered a reliance on caffeine to get you moving in the mornings, removing this part of your eating regimen can really assist you with feeling more invigorated over the long haul and permit your body to assimilate more iron.

Improving utilization of food varieties plentiful in vitamin B12, folates, and L-ascorbic acid is one more accommodating method for getting more iron. If our bodies are having a hard time absorbing iron, whether we are eating enough or not, then health problems are doomed to arise.

Next, it very well may be essential to keep away from lead or lead-containing parts. On the off chance that you are working in a climate where you have openness to lead, this could seriously affect your life and make it challenging to stay away from iron deficiency. This is especially evident assuming you are regularly close to batteries, paint, or petrol, or eat with dishes that contain lead in them.

A decent method for getting more iron in your eating regimen by making a basic way of life change
is to begin cooking with cast-iron pots and pans. Unfortunately, however, cast iron utensils have been known to contain lead. The lead was used to soften the cast iron for molding. If you are cooking with older cast iron pots and pans, it is more likely that they contain lead substances. You can get

these tested to make sure that what you are using to cook with and eat from is actually healthy for the body. Otherwise, you may find yourself at risk of neurological disorders and other conditions.

Another important tip is to look carefully at the ingredients in the foods that you eat. If a food contains the preservative EDTA then it is dangerous to the body and may actually make it more difficult to absorb iron. You should also try to avoid excessive amounts of fiber or calcium in the diet.

It is Also useful to try to pair iron-rich foods with foods that assist in the absorption of iron. The recipes section at the end of this book will touch upon a few ideas that can be utilized. Also, instead of eating types of bread that are made of wheat that has been processed and refined into all-purpose white flour, try opting instead for more grainy bread such as those made of barley or other iron-rich whole grains. It may be an adjustment, but it is one that will serve you well and improve your health, with or without iron deficiency anemia.

Last, but not least, if you are able to find a safe cast-iron pot or pan to cook with, cooking foods in these pans and including acidic and vitamin C-rich ingredients, such as lime or lemon juice, will help your food absorb more iron from this cookware. Not only that, but it will also help your body absorb the iron that the food picks up from the pot and help you to consume more iron than you were receiving before, leading to a higher iron intake overall.

What NOT to Eat When Consuming Iron- Rich Foods

We've spoken a bit about what to eat with iron-rich foods to ensure that as much iron is being absorbed by the body as possible, and we've also touched on things to avoid when taking iron supplements that can inhibit iron absorption in the body. Here is a comprehensive list of things to avoid when eating iron-rich foods to ensure that your body is able to absorb as much iron as possible from the foods that you eat. Wait at least two hours before or after eating iron-rich foods to consume the following.

Do NOT consume the following paired with iron-rich foods:

•Caffeinated beverages

•Soda

•Tea

- Coffee
- Antacids

That isn't to say you should never eat these foods if you have iron deficiency anemia. It simply means that you should time the consumption of these things carefully by making sure that you are not eating any of these caffeine or calcium-rich foods during the time your body is attempting to digest and absorb iron. However, it is recommended to cut down caffeine intake overall to ensure greater absorption of iron into the body.

VEGANS, VEGETARIANS, AND IRON DEFICIENCY

One popular reason that many people might suffer from iron deficiency anemia is a plant-based diet. This lifestyle choice may be undertaken with the best of intentions, but without a real knowledge of nutrition and care for the body and its nutritional needs, a vegan and vegetarian diet may leave you lacking the desired nutrients that promote healthy growth and development.

Vegans are especially prone to the limitations that their diets result in, and iron deficiencies coupled with vitamin B12, folate, and calcium deficiencies may all arise as a serious result of irresponsible diet planning. While it is possible to continue on a path of plant-based eating, it can only be done if care and consideration are taken into the consumption of foods that are diverse and rich in vitamins and minerals that support the metabolic system and other important aspects of the body.

Unfortunately, it is a lot less common for vegans and vegetarians born in North America to have proper nutrition, as the diets that ensure healthy results, such as plant-based diets in countries rich in fruits, vegetables, and whole grains, are not as readily available. The Standard American Diet, also known as the SAD diet, does not prepare most people for a healthy execution of the vegan or vegetarian diets, so one must be entirely self-motivated when it comes to seeing to a nutritionally sound way of approaching this lifestyle.

Iron, Folate, and Vitamin B12 Deficiencies in Vegan and Vegetarian Diets

The sad fact of the matter is that people who live on a plant-based diet for a long time may be neglecting a serious need. Iron, vitamin B12, and folates are generally combined in animal-based foods and consumed together to ensure healthy metabolic systems and blood production. However, once a person decides to embark upon a plant-based diet, that easy source of iron, folates and vitamin B12 are gone.

Without proper nutrition and careful supplementation, nutritional deficiencies can and will occur. The longer you go without diagnosing a nutritional deficiency, the harder it becomes to reverse the results of these dangerous limitations of the body. For example, a vitamin B12 deficiency can permanently reduce brain functioning, harm the memory, and cause lasting damage to the nerves.

These deficiencies are common and often ignored. However, just because we are surviving on the diets that we are on does not mean that our bodies are thriving. And issues later on will crop up, as a result, sometimes even leading to premature death. Take care of your body now rather than suffering later.

How Much Vitamin B12 and Folate Do We Need?

Unless we are deficient in vitamin B12, the amount of this vitamin that we need is surprisingly small. The FDA suggests that we need only consume about 2.4 micrograms of vitamin B12 daily.

What many vegans forget to take into consideration is that the vitamin B12 and folate compound actually work together as part of the B-complex vitamins. Whether or not we consume folic acid won't matter if we aren't receiving enough vitamin B12 to activate it.

It is generally rare to have a vitamin B12 deficiency, but if a plant-based lifestyle is your choice, it is sadly simple. As we age, however, this deficiency can become a lot more common, as our bodies begin to have a hard time absorbing vitamin B12 the older we get. Instead of absorbing the vitamin B12 we receive, we end up eliminating it as a waste product. As for folates, the recommended daily allowance is as follows:

•Children six months old and younger: 65 micrograms per day

•Children seven months to 12 months of age: 80 micrograms per day

•Children one to three years of age: 150 micrograms per day

•Children four to eight years of age: 200 micrograms per day

•Children nine to 13 years of age: 300 micrograms per day

•Children 14 years of age and older: 400 micrograms per day

•Women who are nursing: 500 micrograms per day

•Women who are pregnant: 600 micrograms per day

If a deficiency is found, your doctor may recommend a higher dosage of a folate supplement. Make sure to follow instructions closely in order to combat folate deficiencies before any long-term harm is done to your body or mind.

Symptoms of Vitamin B 12 Deficiency

There are many complications that can arise from a vitamin B12 deficiency. Make sure that you are on top of all of your symptoms and consult a doctor and nutritionist when experiencing symptoms of a vitamin B12 deficiency. Remember, this type of deficiency can make it difficult, if not impossible, to absorb enough iron in the body. Our bodies are made up of systems that work together to function and if one or more areas fail to thrive, that can have a lasting impact on our bodies and minds.

Symptoms of vitamin B12 deficiency include:

•Megaloblastic anemia

•Fatigue

•Pale skin

•Weakness

•Heart palpitations

- Constipation
- Gas
- Vision loss
- Memory loss
- Behavioral changes
- Loss of appetite
- Shortness of breath
- Nerve issues
- Tingling in the arms or legs
- Depression
- Confusion
- Diarrhea
- Shortness of breath

Vitamin B12 deficiency can generally be treated, even if you choose to maintain your vegan or vegetarian lifestyle. If you are not absorbing vitamin B12 as a result of other health problems, that can also generally be treated. For those suffering from health issues outside of their chosen diet, a lifetime of supplements, injections, and nasal therapies meant to help maintain a balance of vitamin B12 can result in a healthier relationship with vitamin B12 for your body.

If you are vegan or vegetarian, a vitamin B12 deficiency is easy to combat and prevent in the future, simply by making conscious dietary choices to include vitamin B12 into your diet. There are supplements, vitamins, and injections that are available to those deficient in vitamin B12 and you should take care to include foods that have been fortified with vitamin B12 so that you do not become deficient in vitamin B12 again.

While these are great ways to work through the symptoms of a vitamin B12 deficiency, there is a sad and lasting problem that cannot always be mended. If the vitamin B12 deficiency was caught too late and caused nerve damage to your body, that is irreversible.

If you suspect you may be suffering from a vitamin B12 deficiency, do everything in your power to get a handle on it and reverse the effects before it is too late. Consult a doctor and be careful when making dietary choices in the future.

HEMOCHROMATOSIS

On the opposite end of the spectrum is an issue known as hemochromatosis. Hemochromatosis is a hereditary condition that makes it difficult to regulate the amount of iron in the body. It usually leads to the over-absorption of iron in the body, which can cause health problems, especially later on in life. Hemochromatosis has several drawbacks and can require a low-iron diet, such as a vegan diet, in order to cope with these symptoms.

What is Hemochromatosis?

Hemochromatosis is the polar opposite of iron deficiency anemia. Instead of making it difficult for the body to absorb iron, it makes it far too easy. Excess iron eventually begins to accumulate within the body, where it is stored in inconvenient locations, such as in the heart, pancreas, or liver. When these organs are burdened by excess stores of iron, it can cause many complications.

Iron is generally absorbed through the intestines and continues to increase the stores of iron in the body that are received through dietary consumption of iron. Unfortunately, because the iron is absorbed rather than expelled through the intestines, it is virtually impossible for people suffering from hemochromatosis to get rid of the excess iron in their bodies.

The body begins to store the iron in the areas mentioned above, with areas such as the adrenal glands, gonads, and joints also being affected. Complications include cirrhosis, lack of adrenaline, diabetes, heart failure, and poly-arthropathy.

When you are diagnosed with hemochromatosis, you are not likely to be given iron supplements of any kind, as this can result in a toxic overload that would prove fatal to a person suffering from this disorder.

Symptoms of Hemochromatosis

Hemochromatosis can be difficult to pinpoint until later on in life when symptoms become more severe. Early warning signs were mentioned previously in the book, but we will mention them here again, with a few more included.

Warning signs and symptoms of hemochromatosis include:

- Fatigue
- Incontinence
- Joint pain
- Bone pain
- Insulin resistance
- Congestive heart failure
- Malaise
- Lethargy
- Adrenal gland damage
- Lack of adrenaline
- Abnormal heart rhythms
- Erectile dysfunction
- Liver cirrhosis or jaundice
- Decreased libido
- Hypogonadism
  - Arthritis, particularly in the knee, shoulder, and the second and third MCP joints in the hands
- Organ damage

Less frequently, symptoms and complications may also include:

- Susceptibility to disease
- Deafness
- Pituitary and parathyroid gland dysfunction
- Dark or gray colored pigmentation of the skin
- Hair loss
- Hypothyroidism
- Osteoporosis

Overall, while the symptoms of hemochromatosis may be difficult to catch early on, the more damage this disease does over time, the more dangerous it can become.

Treating Hemochromatosis

Hemochromatosis, while a complex genetic disease, is also one that can be lived with, using specific methods of keeping this disorder in check. If caught early, you have a much higher chance of preventing some of the more dangerous side effects of toxic iron buildup in the body and organs.

Treatments such as the application of desferrioxamine mesylate and bloodletting can be utilized in order to help remove excessive iron stores to the blood. You may also be instructed to change your diet to one that is less rich in iron and the components that aid in the absorption of iron.

For example, you will want to limit foods listed previously that are rich in vitamin C, and avoid alcohol, red meat, and seafood. The foods that limit iron absorption should be utilized, such as black and tannin-rich teas and calcium.

It can seem bleak to live with hemochromatosis. However, just do your best and listen to your doctors. While there can be some complications, it is possible to live a comfortable life with this condition, especially when it is caught early on.

LOW-IRON RECIPE IDEAS FOR SUFFERERS OF HEMOCHROMATOSIS

People who suffer from hemochromatosis may find that their options seem somewhat limited when they are reduced to trying to live on a low-iron diet. Most people are used to being able to eat meat whenever they want to, and the complications that can arise from hemochromatosis can be varied and significant, depending upon the specific conditions your body is facing.

The recipes and ideas in this chapter are not going to be useful for everybody. Many people with hemochromatosis also suffer from diseases that already have specific dietary restrictions, such as type 2 diabetes. Please use common sense and consult your doctor or nutritionist before implementing any of these ideas into your lifestyle.

It isn't so bad to eat a low-iron diet once you get the hang of it, so hopefully, with these ideas and tips in mind, you will find it somewhat easier to cope with hemochromatosis and still enjoy foods that you thought you would miss when you were diagnosed with hemochromatosis.

Breakfast Recipe: Homemade Low-Iron Cereal

Serving Size: 1

Prep Time: 6 minutes
Cook Time: N/A

Ingredients

- 1 cup shredded wheat, Trader Joe brand
- 1 tsp. cinnamon
- 1 tsp. stevia

- 1 banana
- ¼ cup rhubarb
- 1 tsp. already brewed black tea
- Whole milk

Instructions

1. Mix all dry ingredients together in a medium-sized bowl.

2. Pour in whole milk (use your own discretion here) and add 1 tsp. of black tea.

3. Mix thoroughly and enjoy!

Lunch Recipe: Low- Iron Chicken Soup

Serving Size: 4

Prep Time: 20 minutes

Cook Time: 30 minutes

Ingredients

- 1 lb. pure white chicken breast
- 2 carrots
- 1 onion
- 3 tomatoes
- 1 stick celery
- ½ cup sour cream
- 1 cup water
- 2 boiled eggs
- ½ cup already brewed black tea
- 1 cup shredded cheddar cheese

Instructions

1. Bring a cup of water and a half cup of black tea to a boil.

2.In the meantime, shred chicken and chop vegetables.

3.Place chicken in the broth once boiling and allow to cook for 15 minutes.

4.After 15 minutes, add in the vegetables, boiled eggs, and half of your sour cream.

5.Allow to cook for another 15 minutes. Serve hot and top with sour cream and shredded cheese.

Dinner Recipe: Low- Iron Turkey Chili

Serving Size: 3

Prep Time: 20 minutes

Cook Time: 45 minutes

Ingredients

- 8 oz. ground turkey
- 6 oz. can of kidney beans
- ¼ cup diced onions
- ½ cup already brewed black tea
- 6 oz. diced tomatoes
- 3 oz. tomato paste
- ½ tsp. red pepper flakes
- 2 tsp. olive oil
- Salt and pepper to taste

Instructions

1.Heat a saucepan over medium heat. Pour in the oil and allow to get hot.

2.Once hot, fry the onion until golden brown and translucent.

3.Add the meat and cook with the onions until brown.

4.Pour in diced tomatoes and tomato paste. Mix and allow the combination to simmer for about 10 minutes.

5.Add in the brewed black tea, spices, and kidney beans.

6. Allow to come to a boil before covering and turning the heat on low. 7. Simmer together for half an hour and then serve hot.

Snack Recipe: Matcha Smoothie

Serving Size: 2

Prep Time: 5 minutes

Cook Time: 3 minutes

Ingredients

- 1 banana
- ½ cup frozen raspberries
- ½ cup frozen blueberries
- 1 cup already brewed matcha tea
- 1 tbsp. already brewed black tea
- 5 ice cubes

Instructions

1. Place all ingredients into a high-speed blender.
2. Blend on high until smooth.
3. Serve immediately.

Tips

Unfortunately, it is not good for people with hemochromatosis to eat red meat that is full of iron, or starchy pasta and breads that are made with grains containing iron, so it can seem like options are limited. However, there may be some recipes available that accommodate your specific dietary restrictions if you look into raw vegan cooking.

Another option for hemochromatosis sufferers is to look into vegan cookbooks and consult your doctor. There are often cookbooks readily available for those who are diagnosed with hemochromatosis, so don't be afraid to ask. It can be a difficult diet to get accustomed to.

Last but not least, because hemochromatosis is a genetic condition, make sure that you are adamant about getting your children and other family members tested if it turns out that you are suffering from hemochromatosis. Even though it is not detected until later in life, that is only because of the complications this condition can cause. Be responsible and share your knowledge of this condition with your friends and family members. Remember, knowledge is power!

IRON-RICH RECIPES FOR VEGANS AND VEGETARIANS

Eating a plant-based diet can be hard enough without having to worry about deficiencies everywhere you look. Unfortunately, the fact of the matter remains that you will probably have to be willing to take iron and vitamin B12 supplements if you pursue a plant-based diet.

That being said, it is still possible to enjoy living life to the fullest and enjoying the foods that you eat. Making sure that you eat nutrient-rich foods that help you to prevent the depletion of vitamins and minerals in your body can help to ensure that no matter what you are eating, you are full of vital life energy and ready to take on the world.

Deficiencies in iron and vitamin B12 can leave the brain feeling murky and cloudy, but utilizing the following recipes and tips will allow you to continue living a vegan or vegetarian lifestyle without having to compromise your ethical values for your health and nutrition needs.

Breakfast Recipe: Cinnamon Sugar Quinoa with Raisins

Serving Size: 2

Prep Time: 10 minutes

Cook Time: 10 minutes

Ingredients

- 1 cup quinoa
- 2 cups water
- ¼ cup agave nectar
- 1 tbsp. cinnamon
- 1 tbsp. raisins
- 1 tbsp. roasted almonds

Instructions

1. Bring water to a boil.
2. Add quinoa and stir until all water is absorbed.
3. Stir in cinnamon and raisins.
4. Pour into a serving bowl and top with agave nectar and roasted almonds.
5. Serve immediately.

Lunch Recipe: Iron- Rich Edamame Salad

Serving Size: 2

Prep Time: 10 minutes

Cook Time: N/A

Ingredients

- 1 cup edamame
- 1 cup spinach
- 1 cup kale
- 1 mandarin orange, peeled and separated into pieces
- ½ cup walnuts

- ¼ cup shredded carrot

Instructions

1.Combine all ingredients together in a large salad bowl. 2.Top with shredded carrots and walnuts.

3.Serve immediately.

Dinner Recipe: Iron- Rich Vegetarian Chili

Servings: 6

Prep Time: 12 hrs. 15 minutes

Cook Time: 30 minutes

Ingredients

- 4 oz. lentils
- 4 oz. kidney beans
- 3 oz. black-eyed peas
- 2 cups textured vegetable protein
- 2 cups water
- 1 carrot
- 5 tomatoes
- 1 zucchini
- 1 onion
- 1 tsp. red pepper flakes
- 1 tsp. cumin
- 1 tsp. sweet chili powder

Instructions

1.Soak the beans and lentils for 12 hours or overnight to make it easier for the body to digest them.

2.Chop up the onion, zucchini, tomatoes, and carrot.

3.Add all ingredients into a slow cooker (or boil them together over medium heat for approximately four hours and 30 minutes).

4.Allow cooking in the slow cooker on high heat for two hours.

5.Serve immediately.

Snack Recipe: Vegan Kale Chips

Serving Size: 6

Prep Time: 10 minutes

Cook Time: 15 minutes

Ingredients

- 1 batch of organic kale
- 1 tbsp. extra virgin coconut oil
- 1 tbsp. nutritional yeast flakes
- 1 tsp. salt

Instructions

1.Preheat your oven to 350 degrees Fahrenheit.

2.Chop up your kale into bite-sized pieces. Wash it well and dry before baking.

3.Place kale on a cookie sheet lined with parchment paper. Pour melted coconut oil over the kale and then sprinkle with nutritional yeast flakes and salt.

4.Heat for 15 minutes, until edges are fresh and brown.

5.Serve immediately.

Tips

If you are living with a lack of iron, which is extremely normal on a veggie lover or vegan diet, or then again assuming you are just expecting to keep lack of iron paleness from occurring in your life because of your way of life, it is important

that you can eat the right kinds of foods.

As referenced beforehand, don't combine iron-rich food varieties with food varieties that can repress the ingestion of iron into your body. This can be extremely perilous for you, especially when you are having an adequately hard time in getting the iron that you really want from your eating routine. A decent method for ensuring you are getting sufficient iron from these food sources is to ensure that you are isolating the time you eat these iron-rich food varieties from the times you are eating food sources loaded with calcium. Ensure these pieces of time are isolated by something like two hours when eating iron for the greatest effect of iron absorption.

For the best outcomes, ensure that you are eating in a brilliant manner. Use foods in good combinations, such as eating iron-rich foods paired with foods that are full of vitamin C. Here is a rundown of food varieties that make great sets with iron-rich food varieties, like lentils, mixed greens, and beans.

- Tomatoes

- Squash

- Broccoli

- Citrus

- Foods plentiful in nutrient B12

- Foods rich in folate

If you eat responsibly, then you will be able to avoid issues with iron absorption in your body. Regardless of whether you have effectively demonstrated inadequate in iron or vitamin B12 and folates, or you are essentially wanting to stay away from the most dire outcome imaginable from occurring, there are as yet extraordinary choices for veggie lovers and veggie lovers to partake in their weight control plans nevertheless hold immovably to their moral standing.

Although it very well may be hazardous to carry on with a way of life that makes it hard to get satisfactory sustenance, there are many enhancements out there that can assist you with settling on the decision to be veggie lover or vegan capably, without experiencing the unfavorable wellbeing impacts, like iron lack. In any case, you must be inflexible regarding maintaining the dietary requirements and requests that your body will make on you. Any other way, you will have no one to blame except for yourself for the outcomes of carrying on with your life in an undesirable way.

Many could think it is a moronic decision to carry on with a veggie lover or vegan way of life due to the wellbeing gambles with it might present, yet there is not an obvious explanation to falter assuming you will look past these risks and walk the additional mile to guarantee that you are just about as sound as possible.

IRON-RICH RECIPES AND TIPS FOR MEAT-EATERS

Possibly the most common type of diet that people in North America follow to is a meat-based diet. Fortunately, most red meats are high in iron, B12, and folate, so eating red meat is a great way to help to combat lack of iron pallor. While it can in any case be dangerous when weakness is brought about by other special conditions, there are a few incredible plans and food blends that can be used by individuals who are wanting to forestall and battle lack of iron anemia.

Breakfast Recipe: Iron- Rich Spinach and Bacon Omelet

Serving Size: 2

Prep Time: 5 minutes

Cook Time: 10 minutes

Ingredients

•5 huge eggs

•1 cup spinach

- 1 tomato
- 3 strips bacon
- 1 tbsp. olive oil

Instructions

1. Preheat the oil in a skillet over medium heat.

2. Beat eggs and wash and shred spinach, and wash and dice tomato.

3. Once the oil is hot, fry bacon until fresh and eliminate from heat.

4. Mix spinach and tomato into the egg hitter and afterward fill the skillet.

5. Allow cooking until firm on the base, around four minutes.

6. As it cooks, dice the singed bacon.

7. Flip the omelet over and permit to broil until a covering develops.

8. Place the bacon in the omelet and afterward crease the omelet in half.

9. Allow to sear on the two sides uniformly until

brilliant brown. 10. Serve immediately.

Lunch Recipe: Iron- Rich Potato and Beef Stew

Serving Size: 6 servings

Prep Time: 20 minutes

Cook Time: 30 minutes

Ingredients

- 1 lb. beef
- 5 potatoes
- 5 carrots
- 12 oz. lentils
- 1 onion
- 1 tbsp. olive oil

- 6 cups water

Instructions

1. In a skillet, heat a tablespoon of olive oil.

2. Dice onions.

3. Fry the onions until brilliant brown and clear.

4. Fry the hamburger until browned.

5. Once got done, strip potatoes and wash completely. Dice them into scaled down pieces and set aside.

6. Fill a soup pot with six cups of water.

7. Pour in all fixings, including the oil from cooking the meat and onions.

8. Cover the pot and carry the water to a boil.

9. Once bubbling, decrease to a stew and permit to cook for around 20 minutes.

10. Remove from hotness and afterward serve hot.

Dinner Recipe: Iron- Rich Steak and Potato Dinner

Serving Size: 2 servings

Prep Time: 1 hour and 15 minutes

Cook Time: 20 minutes

Ingredients

- 1 16 oz. steak
- 3 cloves of garlic
- 1 cup of soy sauce
- 2 potatoes
- 1 head of broccoli
- 1 tbsp. olive oil
- 1 tsp. butter

•Salt and pepper to taste

Instructions

1.In an enormous compartment, pour

soy sauce. 2.Peel and mince garlic.

3.Place the steak in the soy sauce and empty the garlic into the holder. Permit marinating for 60 minutes (longer if you prefer).

4.When the steak is adequately marinated, wash potatoes and cut huge cuts in the focal point of them. Prepare for 40 minutes.

5.In a huge skillet, heat the olive oil over medium-high heat.

6.Fry the steak over medium hotness. Flip when brilliant brown on the base and permit to cook the whole way through until steak comes to the ideal consistency.

7.Remove from hotness and put away. Utilize the steak oil to sear the broccoli until radiant green or to your favored texture.

8.Once potatoes are done, top with margarine and serve immediately.

Dessert Recipe: Iron- Rich Roasted Pumpkin Seeds

Serving Size: 2 servings

Prep Time: 10 minutes

Cook Time: 45 minutes

Ingredients

•2 cups crude pumpkin seeds

•2 ½ tsp. liquefied butter
•1 tsp. cinnamon

•1 tsp. nutmeg

•1 tsp. earthy

colored sugar

Instructions

1.Preheat broiler to 300 degrees Fahrenheit.

In an enormous blending bowl, consolidate all fixings together. 2.Stir until completely combined.

3.Pour the pumpkin seeds onto a baking sheet that is fixed with material paper.

4.Bake the pumpkin seeds at similar temperature for around 45 minutes, or until brilliant brown. Ensure that you mix them each 13 minutes.

5.Serve warm and store in a cool dry container.

Tips

Fortunately for individuals who live on a meat-based diet, it is simpler than it would be for somebody who is veggie lover or vegan to get a satisfactory measure of iron, B12, folate, and calcium. It can in any case be testing assuming low iron is a consequence of other wellbeing issues.

All of the plans above are incredible when collaborated with fixings that are plentiful in vitamin B12 and folate. Make an effort not to eat food varieties wealthy in calcium too early previously or subsequent to eating the iron rich food sources above. This is the most effective way to ensure that iron is promptly ingested into the body utilizing the food varieties that are presented through these recipes.

You can likewise glance through a few cookbooks, remembering the supportive iron-rich fixings and supplement fixings that others use with those that you know are high in iron substance. Like that, you will actually want to appreciate promptly accessible iron-rich food sources that are near the food varieties that

you definitely know and love. It is a decent method for assisting you with getting somewhat more imaginative in the kitchen so you don't need to make a decent attempt to ponder every one of the various ways you can utilize food to assist you with enhancing iron in your diet.

Try to continuously cook your meats and vegetables with cast iron skillets and pots so your food retains additional iron from the cookware. It is an incredible method for improving food sources that are low in iron and give them a lift. A few spots sell squares of iron that you can add to your soup pots or skillet that permit iron to drain into your food varieties. These squares are accessible in various plans and are one more intriguing method for consolidating more iron into your diet.

No matter what you decide to do, do whatever it takes not to get deterred assuming you are experiencing a lack of iron and on second thought address it mindfully. It tends to be challenging to re-train yourself to consider iron a significant piece of your eating regimen, yet assuming you can eat meat and you comprehend the intricate details of iron assimilation in the body, you are well headed to incredible health!

10 STEPS AHEAD

Trying to incorporate a low iron diet into your life can be a challenge, just as it can be challenging to live with an iron deficiency. There are many ins and outs to iron absorption in the body, and unfortunately, if you are having an issue retaining iron, there could be many causes and numerous different complexities related with this.

Lack of iron is one of the main lacks of nutrient in North America and we are lucky that there has been such a lot of examination done to assist us with seeing exactly being iron inadequate. Whenever we are adapting to a lack in the body, it can prompt a huge number of issues. Our bodies are exceptionally proficient frameworks and when one thing turns out badly, it can regularly be the start of numerous different sorts of problems.

Thankfully, it is generally easy to treat and forestall a lack of iron in the event that the essential driver of the inadequacy is diet-based. Different kinds of weakness can be more intricate, however they are additionally effortlessly managed through supplements and other dietary changes. Individuals who figure out that they are not engrossing sufficient iron, or who are retaining an excess of iron, may need to go through some troublesome way of life changes, however regardless of a trouble in adjusting, it tends to be an exceptionally advantageous progress to make.

Whether you are a veggie lover or vegan whose diet basically needs iron, vitamin B12, and folates, or you are experiencing pallor for another explanation, iron lack is a typical issue that normally doesn't cause enduring harm. Left untreated, nonetheless, frailty and other nutrient inadequacies connected with weakness can turn out to be very dangerous.

Consulting with your PCP is a significant stage during the time spent dealing with lacks of iron or iron over-burden in the body. With the assistance of a certified clinical expert, you will actually want to comprehend the insufficiencies in your eating regimen and manage them in a more inside and out manner that is ensured to assist you with feeling better when possible.

It is critical that you teach yourself too, and ideally, in the wake of perusing this book, you will feel more ready to handle whatever lies ahead from now on, regardless of whether you are attempting to adapt to a lack of iron, iron over-burden, or you essentially need to keep the most dire outcome imaginable from happening to you.

It is feasible to carry on with your life in a sound and remunerating way, regardless of whether you wind up confronting medical issues. Try to constantly remain positive and stay aware of the decisions that you make and what they could mean for your body. Attempt to think 10 strides ahead with regards to your wellbeing. Furthermore regardless of whether it seems like it's past the point of no return, don't get tied up with that negative outlook. There is dependably time to roll out certain improvements and better yourself, for yourself.

No matter where you fall with your wellbeing, information is power and you truly do have the ability to be just about as sound as you might potentially be. Settle on the decisions that are best for your way of life and be arranged 100% of the time to investigate the future, no less than 10 strides ahead. Regardless the future could bring, you can plan yourself and relax because of the way that you are giving your all to be simply the best form that you might conceivably be. On the off chance that you are on your own group, all that will end up fine.